Alexander Warfield Bradford

The Bank of the Commonwealth

The American Exchange Bank and Others

Alexander Warfield Bradford

The Bank of the Commonwealth
The American Exchange Bank and Others

ISBN/EAN: 9783337120054

Printed in Europe, USA, Canada, Australia, Japan

Cover: Foto ©Suzi / pixelio.de

More available books at **www.hansebooks.com**

Court of Appeals,

STATE OF NEW YORK.

THE BANK OF THE COMMONWEALTH,
THE AMERICAN EXCHANGE BANK AND OTHERS,

APPELLANTS,

against

THE TAX COMMISSIONERS, &c., OF NEW YORK,

RESPONDENTS.

ARGUMENT OF

ALEXANDER W. BRADFORD.

Albany, January 13, 1864.

NEW YORK:
ROBERT CRAIGHEAD, CAXTON BUILDING,
81, 83, AND 85 CENTRE STREET.
1864.

Argument

OF

ALEXANDER W. BRADFORD.

MAY IT PLEASE THE COURT: This is a proceeding for
the correction of the assessment roll for the year 1863, in
the hands of the Commissioners of Taxes and Assessments for the City and County of New York, in relation
to the assessment of the Bank of the Commonwealth, a
banking association transacting business in the City of
New York. A similar proceeding was instituted by The
American Exchange Bank, and other banking associations in New York, which I represent on this argument.

These banks, indeed all the banks interested in this
question, except the Manhattan Company, were formed
under the general banking law of 1838.

The Commissioners of Taxes and Assessments derived
their official powers under chapter 302 of the laws of
1859. By the 10th and 11th sections of that act, they
are authorized, upon application by any person consi-

dering himself aggrieved by the assessed valuation of his real or personal estate, to correct the assessment roll; and it is provided that "if, in their judgment, the assessment is erroneous, they shall cause the same to be corrected." Previous to the passage of this act, the only law governing this subject was the act of 1857, which created the office of Tax Commissioners. Prior to 1857, the whole subject was regulated by the general provisions of the Revised Statutes in relation to the assessment of property liable to taxation by the ward assessors or town assessors throughout the State.

The law of 1857, as modified by the law of 1859, destroyed that system of assessment so far as it related to the city and county of New York, and substituted in the place of ward assessors, twelve Deputy Tax Commissioners, under the direction and control of three Tax Commissioners, who are directed, by the act, to assess all the personal and real property in the city of New York. So that, under the act of 1859, the Deputy Tax Commissioners occupy the place of town assessors in the country, and ward assessors in the several wards, of the cities.

The assessment directed by the act of 1859 is peculiar in another respect : it directs the twelve Deputy Commissioners to assess the whole taxable real and personal estate in the city and county, commencing on the first Monday of September in each year. On the 12th of January, the various corporations of the city of New York liable to taxation are directed to make their returns to the Tax Commissioners. Upon these returns being made, the Tax Commissioners pass upon all claims for exemption from taxation; and, after having rendered their decision, they make up, from the assessments of the Deputy Commissioners as corrected, a book called—"The Book of Annual Record of Taxable Personal and Real Estate in the City and County of New York."

After the book is completed—I say "completed," for if any assessment has been controverted or questioned as erroneous, the Tax Commissioners can correct it,—and, after the corrections are made, and the book is completed, it remains on file as a record of the office of the Commissioners; and it becomes the simple ministerial duty of the Commissioners to copy therefrom the assessment roll, and transmit it to the Board of Supervisors. The assessment roll, therefore, is merely a copy of the Book of Annual Record of the Taxable Real and Personal Property in the City and County of New York.

In sections 10 and 11 of the law of 1859 are contained provisions which authorize the Tax Commissioners to reduce or correct any assessment. Section 20 of the same act provides that a writ of "*certiorari*, to review and correct, on the merits, any decision or action of the said Commissioners under sections 10 and 11," shall be allowed by the Supreme Court.

Your Honors will perceive, when you come to examine the act in question, that the sole duty of the Tax Commissioners is to assess the taxable property in the city of New York. There is no other scope of action under the law except to look at the *property*, in the city and county of New York and give it an assessment or valuation.

The statement of the relators, the Bank of the Commonwealth, in this case, presented to the Tax Commissioners, shows the following state of facts: That the amount of the capital stock of the bank is $750,000 ; amount of property in real estate is $188,089, which, being deducted from the capital, leaves the sum of $561,165 ; and that this amount of personal property the residue of the capital stock, has been loaned to the Government of the United States. Your Honors will perceive, in this connection, that there is a distinct allegation that the whole *capital*, after deducting the value of the real estate, is invested in the securities of the United States Government. Upon some of the returns, which are slightly different in some respects, your Honors will find that there may be some room for doubt whether there is a clear and distinct allegation that all the capital has been invested in government securities. That criticism is made, I believe, by Mr. Justice Sutherland, in the opinion rendered by him, at General Term, in the case of the Bank of Commerce. But here there can be no question made; the allegation is, and it has never been denied, but remains an admitted fact, that the whole capital of this institution, with the exception of the amount invested in real estate, has been loaned to the Government of the United States, and for which the bank has taken and holds the securities of the United States in stocks, bonds, notes, evidences of debt, and securities for money ; and they therefore claim that the amount so loaned and invested in the securities of the United States is exempt from taxation by and under the Constitution and laws of the United States, and by and under the decision and judgment of the Supreme Court of the United States; thereby referring, in the most obvious manner, to the recent decisions upon that subject in the Supreme Court of the United States.

The Commissioners, upon these claims of exemption from taxation being made, refused to allow any exemption of the amount thus invested; and this decision was sustained by the Supreme Court at General Term. The return of the Commissioners to the writ of *certiorari*, to review their decision, in which their action is set forth in detail, is, in some respects, worthy of particular observation and comment. It will be found on page fourteen of the case:

" We, the undersigned, Commissioners of Taxes and Assessments for the City and County of New York, pursuant to a certain writ of *certiorari*, delivered to us, and hereto annexed, do certify and return ——."

. I call your Honors' close attention to what I am about to read, to see what the Commissioners did, and under what law the Commissioners appear to have acted:

"That the Deputy Tax Commissioners did, under our direction, as by law required, assess *the actual value* of the *capital stock* of the Bank of the Commonwealth, after *deducting* the assessed value of its real estate, *and all shares of stocks in other corporations* actually owned by such company which are liable to taxation upon their stock under the laws of this State, and amount of stock held by *charitable and literary institutions*, at the sum of five hundred and sixty-one thousand nine hundred dollars ($561,900) —."

That is the amount upon which we claim exemption.

" — and that such *assessed valuation* was duly entered at detail in the books provided for that purpose, and kept in the office of the said Commissioners, called 'The Annual Record of the Assessed Valuation of Real and Personal Estate,' as appears by the extract hereunto annexed, marked 'B.' That notice of such assessment was given to said bank ; that thereupon the officers of said bank did appear before us, and did complain of said assessment, and did present to us certain statements in writing, of which a true copy is hereunto annexed, marked 'A.'

"That thereupon we, the said Commissioners, did examine into the said complaint, and, in our judgment, the said assessment was, and is correct, and we determined that the *actual value* of the said capital stock, after making the aforesaid *deductions*, was five hundred and sixty-one thousand and nine hundred dollars, which we believed and now believe to be *just*, and such assessment stands in the said Annual Record of the *Assessed Valuation of Real and Personal Estate* as an assessment for that amount against the said bank."

So far, your Honors will perceive that no allusion is

made to the law of 1863, which, it is claimed, effected an alteration in the right of the Tax Commissioners to tax moneyed corporations having their capital invested in government securities. Having returned that they had assessed the capital stock of this bank at its actual value, they then proceed :

" That said assessment so made, and our action thereupon, were under and in pursuance of the several laws of the State of New York, relating to the assessment and collection of taxes in the city and county of New York.

" And we do further certify and return that the said, The Bank of the Commonwealth, is, and for several years last past has been, a banking corporation, created under and by the laws of the State of New York, and not otherwise ; and under and in pursuance of such laws, enjoys and has, during all said time, enjoyed certain privileges, and is and has been subject to certain burdens; and among other burdens is, and was at the time of such assessment, subject to assessment and taxation upon *the value of its capital stock*, without regard to the fact that such capital stock, or any portion of it, might be invested in the public stocks, debts, or bonds of the United States ; and that such assessment was not made upon the public stocks or bonds of the United States, but was made pursuant to the laws of said State of New York, *upon the capital stock of said bank*, estimated at its *just value*, after making the *exceptions* and *deductions* required by the statutes of said State."

Now, for aught that appears upon this return, every fact there stated comports exactly with the state and condition of the law, as existing after the passage of the act of 1857, to which I shall call your Honors' attention, and under which law the Supreme Court of the United States declared and decided that the capital stock of this bank invested in United States stocks was exempt from taxation.

In the year 1859, before the commencement of the war, and before the discussion of any of those great constitutional questions which have necessarily arisen in the unsettled condition of our country—in a state of peace, and under a statute of this State, passed in 1857, which provides that corporations should be taxed upon the *actual value* of their capital, The Bank of the Commonwealth, the present relators, instituted a similar proceeding on *certiorari* from the Supreme Court to the Tax Commissioners, for the purpose of procuring exemption from taxation upon $103,000 of its capital invested in United States Stocks of the loan of 1858. The law authorized the deposit, by banking associations, of United States securities for the redemption of the bills of the bank. The Tax Commissioners refused to allow the exemption claimed, and their decision was affirmed by the Supreme Court and by the Court of Appeals. The judgment of this Court was reversed by the Supreme Court of the United States in March, 1863. This decision was made without reference to the act of Congress of 1862, declaring that all government stocks should be exempt from taxation. It was made in reference to investments made prior to 1859, by the Bank of the Commonwealth in government stock issued in 1858, and the right of exemption from taxation on these investments was sustained by the supreme national tribunal *under the Constitution* of the United States, and not under the act of Congress of 1862.

The Legislature of this State, shortly after this determination of the Supreme Court of the United States, on the 29th of April, 1863, passed an act, which was signed by the Governor, and took effect as a law on that day. The following is the entire law :

" *An Act in relation to the Taxation of Moneyed Corporations and Associations.*

" Section 1. All banks, banking associations, and other moneyed corporations and associations, shall be liable to taxation, on a valuation equal to the amount of their capital stock, paid in, or secured to be paid in, and their surplus earnings (less ten per cent. of such surplus), in the manner now provided by law, deducting the value of the real estate held by any such corporation or association, and taxable as real estate.

"SECTION 2. This act shall take effect immediately." (Laws of 1862, ch. 240.)

At this point of the argument, I desire to call the attention of the Court to the condition of the laws of the State in respect to the taxation of moneyed corporations.

The general laws in regard to the taxation of banking corporations, as originally contained in the Revised Statutes, remained intact, except so far as related to the voluntary banking system, until the year 1853. That system was simply to assess the banking corporation on the nominal amount of its capital stock. If it had lost anything it could not escape taxation ; if it had increased its capital stock, that increase could not be taxed. The law continued in this position until the year 1853, with regard to general moneyed corporations. In the year 1853, the State first began to tax the surplus profits of the banks. I presume this change in the system of taxation was suggested by a curious case that arose in the city of New York. The Chemical Bank, it is said, had adopted the policy for many years of reserving its surplus funds or profits until they had reached an amount equal to its original capital stock, and upon which there was no taxation.

The Hon. JAMES EMOTT, associate Counsel with Mr. BRADFORD :—"Three times as much as its original stock."

Mr. BRADFORD.—My associate says it was " three times the amount of their original capital stock." So the Legislature of this State, by the act of 1853, taxed the surplus profits of the banks over ten per cent. In 1857, a law was passed which provided that all moneyed corporations should be taxable on the *actual value* of their capital stock, subject to *all legal exemptions ;* and that their *property* should be assessed in the same manner as the other real and personal property in the county. As this law obliterated the old rule of taxing moneyed corporations upon the nominal valuation of their capital stock, and taxed them upon the actual valuation of their capital, the same as an individual, and provided that they should have the same privilege of exemption as in the case of an individual, it became obviously manifest that if a banking association had invested its capital, or a portion thereof, in United States stock which was exempt from taxation, it should be entitled to the exemption the same as in case of an individual who had made such an investment.

On coming with the case of the Bank of the Commonwealth to this Court, the ground seems to have been admitted that if the stock of the bank was exempt from taxation under the Constitution of the United States, the bank was entitled to the benefit of the exemption, both under the Constitution and under the laws of this State. But this Court held that loans to the general Government, whether in the hands of *individuals* or *corporations*, were *not exempt* from taxation unless they had been taxed by way of discrimination, and with the evident intent to affect the loan. On taking that case to the Supreme Court of the United States, that eminent tribunal adopted the idea of this Court, that a banking corporation was entitled, under the act of 1857, *to all the exemptions* to which an individual was entitled; and they came, therefore, to the conclusion that, as an individual was exempt from taxation upon loans to the general Government, so a bank was exempt from taxation upon loans to the general Government.

Immediately upon the heel of that decision, the Legislature of this State passed the act under which it is claimed that the banks are liable to taxation upon their capital and surplus, notwithstanding the investment thereof in loans to the United States.

The question now arises, whether the exemption from taxation upon so much of their capital as the banks have invested in United States stocks, which exemption was declared by the judgment of the Supreme Court of the United States, has been destroyed by this act of posterior State legislation.

PRELIMINARY QUESTION.

There was a preliminary question raised in the Court below, which, I suppose, will again be presented here, to this effect: that the relators are not within the provisions of the act giving the benefit of the writ of *certiorari* to review the decision of the Tax Commissioners; and that, if the relators are correct in their claim of exemption from taxation, the proceeding should have been instituted against the Board of Supervisors. I am satisfied that from merely a cursory examination of the statute, your Honors will readily conclude that this position is not tenable. I will, therefore, not dwell upon it farther than to mention the answers to the objection.

To this proposition we reply, First: That the duty of the Board of Supervisors is simply ministerial, and in no respect judicial. The only duty of the Board is to apportion the tax, authorized to be raised, among the several tax-payers, according to the valuations contained in the assessment roll. They have nothing to do with the assessment or valuation of the property. The error of which we complain, lies in the assessment of property not taxable, and not in the *apportionment* of the tax by the Supervisors upon the property returned by the Commissioners as taxable.

Second. The duty of the Tax Commissioners is *quasi* judicial; and for that reason the writ of *certiorari* was given to review, and, if necessary, correct their decision.

It is true the issuing of the writ effects a stay of proceedings; but the stay applies only to the particular assessment, and not to the entire assessment roll.

My learned opponent had, in the Court below, an argument of inconvenience as to the effect of a stay of proceedings in respect to delay in collecting the tax, and expense growing out of a multitude of suits; but this would apply equally to proceedings by way of *mandamus* against the Board of Supervisors. We submit, however, that even if the remedy were not given by the act, the decision of the Tax Commissioners being judicial, a common law writ of *certiorari* would lie, and be an appropriate remedy to correct their determination; and upon this point I refer the Court to the cases in Abbot's Digest, title *certiorari*. It was urged, however, that the act of 1859 gave the remedy to correct an erroneous decision of the Tax Commissioners only to persons aggrieved, and not to *corporations*. To this I reply that corporations, though *artificial* persons, are to be treated as *persons* under the general provisions of the tax laws, except where the context indicates otherwise. That is no modern rule; it was applied as long ago as 1823, when this very question was raised that corporations were not persons, and therefore did not come within the operation of the laws relative to taxation. The Supreme Court held that the general provisions of the laws in respect to taxation applied as well to corporations as to persons. (The People *vs.* Utica Insurance Co., 11 John. R., 358, 382; Citing Clinton Woolen Co. *vs.* Morse, Supreme Court, 1824. Ontario Bank *vs.* Burwell, 10 Wendell, 186.) Moreover it would seem to be a sound rule, upon general principles, that as the statute provides the means of assessing corporations as well as individuals, the right to the remedy to correct an unjust or erroneous decision must be equally applicable to both. It cannot be in the nature of things that, where a statute has provided means of levying taxes upon corporations and individuals, the writ which is remedial shall be restricted to one, and not allowed to the other. Your Honors will find upon reference to the act, that "person" and "party" are convertible terms; and the law undoubtedly intended that any "party" interested should be entitled to the benefit of this writ by way of appeal. Leaving this technical question, I invite your Honors' attention to the merits of the main question, and the highly important principles involved in this case.

FIRST. My first proposition is, that since the decision of the Supreme Court of the United States, the supreme tribunal in all cases involving the supremacy of the Constitution of the United States over State legislation, there can no longer remain a doubt that *the power of the general Government to borrow money upon* the *faith* and *credit of the United States cannot in any way be impaired or affected by State taxation.* I say, cannot *in any way* be impaired or affected by State taxation, and that there is no possible mode of reaching that result. This is the position I intend to maintain. And further, I respectfully submit that, in view of our obligations to the National Government, the decisions of the State Courts

should, in all cases, conform not only to the rule laid
down by the supreme tribunal, but also to the principles and grounds upon which that rule is based; and the
same proposition is applicable to all State legislation,
that it should not only conform to the rule in its formal
and technical dimensions, but also to the grounds and
principles upon which the rule has been founded and
enunciated in all their most ample dimensions; not merely to the letter, but to the spirit and intent; and finally,
that it is incumbent upon this high tribunal, whenever the
State Legislature may seem in any respect to have passed beyond the line of Constitutional duty to the Government of the United States in matters which have been
considered and decided by the Supreme Court, to apply
the law as determined by that Court, not with any
narrow and technical views, but with a broad and gene-
rous regard to the spirit of the decision, and the principles at issue. I respectfully submit that, if this is an
obligation incumbent upon the Courts of the States, it is
to be executed and carried out with unsparing certainty.
If, at any time, it appears to come in contact with any
apparent State interests, the latter should succumb and
be entirely disregarded. The National Constitution, and
its judicial interpretation by the Supreme Court, being
the supreme law of the land, wherever State legislation
falls short of Constitutional obligations, it becomes the

high and solemn duty of the State Judiciary to interpose. It gives me great pleasure to state, that I believe the Court of Appeals has conformed to this view in the previous tax cases which have come before this Court since the decision of the Supreme Court of the United States, and have done so cheerfully and heartily, and not grudgingly.

SECOND. The rule in respect to the question of State taxation, as laid down by the Supreme Court of the United States, imparts, to the power of the general Government to borrow money, *complete immunity*. The line of argument on that point, is briefly this : Congress has power to levy armies, build navies, establish post-offices, coin money, regulate trade and commerce, and *borrow money upon the credit of the United States*. This power to borrow money is one of the means essential to the existence of the government theoretically, and, as it has recently been very clearly evinced, practically. It is a power, the exercise of which is just as much removed from State control as is the post-office, or the mint, or the navy, or the army of the United States. In other words, *it is not the subject of State sovereignty*, because it is one of the means of carrying on the National Government, which, within the line of its functions and powers, is supreme over all State Governments, and is so declared

by the express letter of the National Constitution. In
the cases of The Bank of the Commonwealth and The
Bank of Commerce, to which I have referred, the Supreme Court of the United States held, in view of this
principle, that the question whether Government loans
were subject to State taxation or were free, was not
affected by the fact that no selection was made, and they
were taxed only in the aggregate with the tax-payers'
other property, nor upon the fact that there was no discrimination burdensome to this class of property. But the
Court placed the exemption from State taxation on the
ground of NATIONAL SOVEREIGNTY; that the power to
borrow money was one of the means of government; and
that the stock which represented the loan, when effected,
was not within the scope of State authority, and could
not in any way be touched; that, being in existence by
virtue of a Constitutional exercise of the National Sovereignty, it was beyond the dominion of the State of New
York, and could not, in any respect, become the subject
of State Sovereignty.

[Recess to 4 o'clock, P.M.]

The Court reassembled at 4 P.M.

MR. BRADFORD resumed:—In making the remarks
that I have made, and that I am about to make, in re-

gard to the decision of the Supreme Court of the United States, in the cases of The Bank of Commerce and The Bank of the Commonwealth, I do not desire to be understood as not treating those cases as decisive of the rule of law upon the subject; but I feel the propriety, if not necessity, of expounding the reasons and grounds of the decision, to see how far they are applicable to the questions now presented to the Court, and how far they may be avoided or affected by the act of the State Legislature under which it is claimed the Tax Commissioners have proceeded.

I maintain the proposition that the rule, as judicially declared, imparts a *complete immunity* to the power of the Government to borrow money : first, from any *direct* interference by the States; for example, any legislative prohibition to the people of the State to lend to the Government; second, from any direct or *indirect* interference by the States, in respect to the money loaned, or to be loaned, or the certificates or evidences of indebtedness.

State taxation, whether directly or indirectly made, is an interference with this immunity, and is, therefore, unconstitutional and void. The sole and absolute ground upon which the Supreme Court of the United States

placed the cases of McCullough *vs.* The State of Maryland, and Weston *vs.* The City of Charleston, was this :
Taxation involves the power to destroy; it proceeds from
a *sovereign* power which, if it can be exercised in the
slightest degree, can be exercised in any degree. The
question between the Government of the United States
and the State Governments, therefore, is not as to the
extent, or as to the *mode*, in which the State sovereignty
can be asserted over the power of the general Government to borrow money ; but it is as to the very thing
itself, *res ipsa.* The power of the general Government,
as enunciated by the Constitution, is *supreme*, and is
therefore exempt wholly, thoroughly, and entirely from
any, even the slightest interference of the State sovereignty. We are, therefore, delivered totally from the
inquiry as to the *mode* of taxation, or as to the *extent* of
taxation. The inquiry must be simply—*Is this a tax ?*
and if the reply be affirmative, then the immunity springs
up, flowing from the sovereign power of the United
States Government in all matters where, under the Constitution, it has been clothed with authority by the people. Your Honors will, therefore, perceive that this
immunity is a *complete* immunity, and not partial; it is a
real immunity, not nominal; it is an immunity which is
effective for all the purposes for which it is declared. It
protects the money loaned to the Government; it pro-

tects the evidences or securities of debt given by the
Government. It declares that the Government shall be a
borrower, without let or hindrance from State authority;
and, in the same breath, it declares that the lender shall
be a lender without any interference from State authority. In both, as a living energy, a vital power, it throws
the shield of the Constitution entirely around the whole
scope and extent of the exercise of all functions of the
general Government. It is a complete panoply to the
borrower, the lender, the money loaned, and the security
given. The whole subject, with all its branches and inci-
dents and accessories, is beyond State sovereignty, and
resides under the protection and dominion of the Constitution of the United States.

It follows, therefore, that whether this tax be rea-
sonable; whether it be indiscriminative; whether it
be on the whole, or on a part of the property; and
whether levied on persons or on corporations, are all
matters of indifference. Taxation upon the credit of the
National Government in any mode, upon any person, or
upon any corporation, is invalid. The *modus* is utterly
indifferent. In whatever way taxation may be accom-
plished, it conflicts with the power of the Government
to borrow money, and that power is supreme. The
effect of this rule, now judicially declared, is to withdraw,

4

or rather to exclude the stocks of the United States entirely from the bulk of taxable property in the States. At the time of the decision of the case of Weston *vs.* The City of Charleston, Mr. Justice Thompson, of the Supreme Court, dissented from the judgment, and in so doing he gave what he understood to be the full scope, measure, and extent of the principle adopted by the Court on that occasion, and he gave it as the reason why he dissented. He stated that he understood the Court to hold that the stock was not the subject of taxation in any form whatever; that, as he interpreted the conclusion of the Court, it was tantamount to saying:

"The stock is not taxable in any shape or manner whatever; it is not to be included in the estimate of property subject to taxation."

(2 Peters's R., 475.)

Mr. CHIEF JUSTICE DENIO, in this Court, in the case of The Bank of the Commonwealth, stated with great exactness, and distinctness, and perspicuity, what the real question at issue involves :

"The question recurs, whether there is anything in the Constitution of the United States which, by a fair interpretation, forbids this State, under the tax laws, from including in the aggregate valuation of the tax-payer's property, in respect of which he is to be taxed, money which he has lent to the Federal Government, for which he holds its evidence of indebtedness."

A most clear statement of the real proposition involved—,and which is answered by the Supreme Court of the United States, in the opinion of Mr. Justice Nelson, in the same case, on appeal, where he says :

"We have a principle, which leaves the power of taxing the people and property of a State unimpaired ; which leaves to a State the command of all its resources (that is, its own resources), and which places beyond its reach all those powers which are conferred by the people of the United States on the Government of the Union, and all those means which are given for the purpose of carrying these powers into execution. We have a principle which is safe for the States, and safe for the Union."

Bank of Commerce *vs.* Tax Commissioners. 25 Howard, Pr. R. p. 9.

Now, the operation and effect of the rule are precisely such as suggested in this opinion. We have a principle which *"places beyond the reach"* of State authority, what ?—*The power of the general Government to borrow money.* " Beyond the reach !" beyond all State sovereignty, all interference or control, and, *inter alia*, beyond all the means and appliances of taxation. This power to borrow money on the credit and faith of the United States is left with the highest attribute of supremacy—freedom. Thus far there would seem to be no difficulty in readily arriving at a just conclusion. But the idea was advanced at an early period of the discussion in the case of The Bank of the Commonwealth, and was presented in each of the tribunals to which the controversy was carried, that the State possesses a sovereign power over corporations ; that corporations, being creations existing simply by virtue of State legislation, they are obligated by every act of the power which created them, whether exercised by way of general taxation or taxation upon their corporate powers or franchise. If this position be sound, then it is urged that, although their property be invested in securities of the United States, they have no right to claim any exemption from the burdens of State taxation.

Now, within the whole scope of this controversy, there is really no ground for serious dispute, except so far as may be afforded by this position in respect to corporations. I maintain, in refutation of it, that *property* is all that is taxable by the laws of the State of New York. Doubtless the Legislature may pass a law placing taxation on corporate franchises, but it will be time enough to consider its effect when such legislation is effected. As the matter now stands, all that is taxable by the laws of the State of New York is *real and personal estate.*

CHIEF JUSTICE DENIO.—Is it your opinion that, if this act had professed in words to tax the franchise, irrespective of the property owned by a corporation, that would have been in violation of the decision of the Supreme Court of the United States?

MR. BRADFORD.—I think so; that is, of the grounds and principles of that decision.

CHIEF JUSTICE DENIO.—You hold that this statute is not to that effect?

MR. BRADFORD.—I do not think it is. It will defy the power and ingenuity of man to levy a tax upon the franchise of a corporation except in two modes. It must be a general tax like a poll-tax, ten dollars a head, or $50,000 a year; or it must be a tax with graduation in respect to property.

CHIEF JUSTICE DENIO.—I mean a tax upon the franchise measured by the capital paid in.

MR. BRADFORD.—Then you tax the franchise according to the amount of property which the party possesses, and that is a tax on property. You must rate it either upon the principle of an arbitrary tax upon the franchise, that is you must rate it as a poll-tax; or you must make it variable, according to the amount of capital originally paid in, or continuing to exist; and then it becomes a tax which varies according to *the amount of property.*

But I take the law as it is ; I do not believe that the State Legislature ever will deliberately place a tax upon the franchise of a corporation, which shall be rated not according to its property, but generally in a gross sum,—in order to accomplish the object of taxing United States securities in avoidance of a decision of the Supreme Court of the United States. I contend, moreover, there are no corporate franchises in this State, in the ordinary signification of the term, as implying a bounty or donation, a special grant or freedom ; but that corporations, under the general corporation act, possess constitutional rights which cannot be made the subject of special taxation.

THIRD. The act of April, 1863, directs that moneyed

corporations shall be taxed in *the manner now provided by law.* We are referred, therefore, to all the existing statutes of the State for the interpretation and application of this act of 1863. Under the general statutes of the State of New York, there is no subject of taxation except "lands" and "personal estate." Nothing is taxed except Property.

(1 R. S. p. 388, § 1.)

The first title of the chapter "of the Assessment and Collection of Taxes," is entitled "of the *property* liable to taxation;" and the first section declares, that "all lands and all personal estate within this State, whether owned by *individuals* or by *corporations*, shall be liable to taxation, subject to the exemptions hereinafter specified." In other words, property is taxable, whether real or personal, and whether owned by individuals or corporations ; no distinction is made as to the ownership ; whether private or corporate, it is all taxable alike.

By the third section, the terms "personal estate," or "personal property," are defined to include "public stocks and stocks in moneyed corporations," and also "such portion of the capital of incorporated companies, liable to taxation on their capital, as shall not be invested in real estate." Here we have an exact definition. It is only *property* that is taxed; taxable *property* consists of two kinds—real and personal; and the words " personal property" are declared to include so much of the capital of incorporated companies liable to taxation on their capital as shall not be invested in real estate. Adhering to this terminology, the consequence is, throughout that statute, wherever we find the phrase " *capital* of a corporation," we must hold it to mean " *property* of a corporation."

The exemptions from taxation show also that it is only *property* which is taxed. By the fourth section it is declared: " The following *property* shall be exempt from taxation: all *property*, real and personal, exempted from taxation by the Constitution of this State, or *under the Constitution of the United States.*" After defining that " personal property" includes " the capital of incorporated companies," the statute proceeds to say, that whatever is exempt from taxation under the Constitution of the United States shall be exempt under the laws of this State; and not making any distinction as to such exemption, whether claimed in behalf of the property of corporations or individuals. I believe, and always have believed, that the Legislature of New York, in enacting this provision in regard to exemptions under the Constitution of the United States, had express reference to the case of Weston *vs.* The City of Charleston, in which the Supreme Court of the United States decided that Government stocks were not the subject of State taxation.

The course of State legislation on this point is worthy of attention. As early as 1813, taxes were laid on all public stocks, including stocks of the United States; that was before the decision was made in the case of McCullough *vs.* The State of Maryland, in which it was held that the Bank of the United States was not taxable. Afterwards, by the laws of 1823, it was provided that all real estate belonging to the United States, and all personal property exempted from taxation by some *law* of the United States, should be exempt from State taxation. This new provision still, however, did not reach the case of exemption *under the Constitution*, without any law. But in 1829, the decision was announced in the case of Weston *vs.* The City of Charleston, in which the Supreme Court held that United States stocks were exempt from State taxation, under the Constitution; and then the change was made from the exemption of property exempted by some *law* of the United States, to the exemption of such property as was free under the *Constitution* of the United States. Your Honors well know that this famous decision proceeded on the ground that, although there was no *law* that exempted the

5

Government stock from State taxation, yet, by the sole vigor of the *Constitution* itself the freedom from taxation existed. This would seem to leave no doubt that the change made on the revision of the Statutes in 1830, to which I have adverted, was made in reference to that very decision, and with a view to conform to it by State legislation.

But to return to the proposition I was discussing—that it is only *property* which is taxable in this State—I submit that the other exemptions provided by the statute assist towards the same conclusion. Thus the following is declared not to be taxable: 1. All *lands* belonging to this State or to the United States. 2. Every *building* erected for the use of a college, incorporated academy, or other seminary of learning ; every building for public worship; every school-house, court-house, and jail, and the several lots whereon such buildings are situated, and the *furniture* belonging to each of them. 3. Every poor-house, alms-house, house of industry, and *every house* belonging to a company incorporated for the reformation of offenders, and the real and personal *property* belonging to or connected with the same. 4. The real and personal *property* of every public library. 5. All *stocks* owned by the State, or by literary or charitable institutions. 6. The personal estate of every *incorporated company*, not made liable to taxation on its *capital.* 7. The *personal property* of every minister of the gospel or priest of any denomination, and the *real estate* of such minister or priest, when occupied by him, provided such real and personal estate do not exceed the value of one thousand five hundred dollars. 8. All *property* exempted by law from execution.

That it is only *property* which is taxable, further appears by the seventh section of the statute, which provides that the owner or holder of any stock in any incorporated company *liable to taxation on its capital,* shall not be taxed as an individual for such stock.

Again, in the second title, as to " the place and manner in which *property* is to be assessed." Section six provides that the real estate of all *incorporated companies* liable to taxation shall be assessed in the town or ward in which the same shall be, in the same manner as the real estate of *individuals;* and all the *personal estate* of every *incorporated company,* liable to taxation on its capital, shall be assessed in the town or ward where the principal office is; language which continues to include, under the term of "personal estate," the property or "capital" of incorporated companies.

That it is only property which is taxable, further appears by the provisions of the fourth title, declaring that "all moneyed or stock corporations deriving an income or profit from their capital, shall be liable to taxation on their capital in the manner" thereinafter described. By the sixth section of this title, the assessors are required to enter upon their assessment rolls "*the property*" of all incorporated companies—namely, the amount of "capital stock" paid in and secured to be paid in. Here we have the exact relation of these terms. The general term or major includes all the particulars. Having required the *property* to be entered on the assessment roll, the statute carefully enumerates the various kinds of property intended—namely, the amount of the capital stock, the amount invested in real estate, the amount belonging to the State, or to incorporated literary, and charitable institutions. So it appears by the very words of the statute, that, independently of profits and investments in real estate, the property of a corporation and the capital stock of a corporation are identically the same thing.

FOURTH. There is a clear and well defined distinction between a tax upon property and a tax upon persons, natural or artificial. There may be a poll or capitation tax; also personal requisitions to perform public duties;

and likewise taxes upon certain acts and trades, or fran-chises by way of license or excise. These are all in their nature essentially different from a tax on property. If levied, they must, of necessity, be fixed at some arbitrary sum ; if not, then they must be rated according to pro-perty, and so would become substantially a tax on pro-perty. Our State has not provided any mode of assess-ing or levying such duties in the provisions relating to the taxation of *property*. If they can be assessed and levied, it must be by some system independent of the method of taxing *property*, contained in the Revised Statutes. For the law, as it now stands, is utterly want-ing in the means of levying and collecting a poll-tax or a tax on corporate franchises ; its provisions relate solely and simply to a tax on property, real and personal; all its machinery is adapted to that single purpose, and none of it can be made effective towards levying or col-lecting any other tax.

FIFTH. It is of no material consequence whether a tax be levied on a person natural or artificial in *respect* to property, or on the *property itself*. Of necessity, the law can act primarily upon the person who is the owner ; that is the most natural, the most easy, and the most effective way of levying a tax, because it affords a double security—the security of the person, and the security of the property. But it is substantially the same thing, in a pecuniary sense, whether the State taxes the owner in respect of the property, or taxes the property itself; as, in each event, the owner loses part of the property. So it is clear that, under any system where property is the criterion of taxation and affords the basis of a rate of assessment, the tax may be said to be a tax upon the property, or a tax upon the person or institution owning it in respect to such property. It is only a different mode of announcing the same proposition. "In this State," citing the opinion of Mr. Justice Comstock, in the case of The Bank of the Commonwealth, which does not appear to have been disputed on this point—"In this State, all taxation is upon *property*. It is the same thing, in substance, to say that it is upon the owner in respect to property."—23. *N. Y. R.* 192.

It is true, there may be a difference in the *mode* of assessing and valuing the property of a person and the property of a corporation. But let us suppose that the mode is the same in each case, according to the determination of Mr. Justice Denio in the case of The Bank of the Commonwealth.

Assuming that the mode of taxing a person and

taxing a corporation is the same—that is, upon the actual value of the property; then, as to exemptions from taxation under the Constitution of the United States, the position of a corporation, to quote the language of Chief Justice Denio, "is precisely the same as that of an individual tax-payer. It is, as a general rule, assessed and taxed for all its property of every kind; but there is an exception as to such part of its property as the Constitution and laws of the Union and of the States have, upon special reasons of policy, declared shall be exempted. Whether such exempt property is found in the hands of an individual, or in the possession of a corporation taxed upon the actual value of its capital, the rule is the same; the exempt property is to be deducted from the aggregate valuation, and the tax is to be imposed on the residue."—23. *N. Y. R.* 192.

CHIEF JUSTICE DENIO.—I was speaking of the act of 1857 then, I think.

MR. BRADFORD.—Yes, sir. Supposing they were taxed upon the actual value, then your Honor said : "The rule is the same; the exempt property is to be deducted from the aggregate valuation, and the tax is to be imposed upon the residue." In other words, assuming that the mode of taxing an individual and of taxing a corporation is the same—that is, upon the actual value of their property—then, in each case, the exempt property must be deducted, and the corporation or individual can only be taxed upon the residue. The single question left, therefore, was for the learned judge to determine whether this property was exempt under the Constitution of the United States.

Sixth. My next proposition is, that the privilege of exemption from taxation on so much property as may have been loaned to the Government of the United States, cannot be made to depend upon *the mode of valuation*, either of the property of an individual or the property of a corporation.

One of the ways in which it is supposed that the immunity of the stock of the Government from taxation can be—I will not say evaded, but avoided or escaped— is for the State to say—We do not tax moneyed corporations upon the money which they have loaned to the general Government, nor upon the stock which they have received in lieu thereof, for that would require an actual valuation; but we tax them upon the property which they *had before* they made that loan—upon its nominal value *at that time*.

Now, if the power of the Government of the United States to borrow money, can be made dependent upon the *manner* in which the State Legislature values the property of a corporation or of an individual, then the power is utterly at the mercy of State Legislation. If the State can by its laws say to a corporation—" We do not tax you upon the money you have loaned to the United States Government, for *you have parted* with *that* money, and it belongs to the general government; we do not tax you upon the security you have taken in lieu thereof from the United States Government, for that is a part of the process and machinery of borrowing money, but we tax you upon the money you *had the instant before you made the loan to the United States*"—then the power of the general government is utter emptiness; its credit is completely worthless, lying exposed to the ingenious methods by which the States may vary the mode of assault.

It is obvious also that the same covered way in which the attack is made on a corporation, may be made on an individual—the State can tax a person on what *he had*, and not on what *he has;* can say, it is true you have loaned your money to the United States, and it is no longer yours, and we cannot tax it, because it belongs to the government, and not to you; we cannot tax the *security* which the government has given you in lieu of your money, but we will tax you upon the nominal value of your property a day, or a week, or a month, before you made the loan. Surely, if such a course be right, and legal, and constitutional, then the freedom of the power of the United States from State taxation depends merely upon modes and forms and names, and not upon substantial ground of principle. But if on the other hand, it be obvious that the effect of such a tax will fall upon the government as an impediment to the power of borrowing money, and if that power is supreme and beyond the reach of State Legislation, then there can be no possible constitutional way of effecting such a result as to make the superior subject to the inferior.

We ask upon what principle is the exemption from taxation maintained?

Simply this: The government has the money of the individual, or of the corporation, by way of loan, and has given security for its return, and if the State tax assessor looks upon the property which the party having made such a loan *now owns*, he finds nothing which is taxable; the security being protected from taxation. If, then, to escape the immunity thus thrown over the security, the assessor be directed not to look to the actual mode of investment, but to its previous condition, and so assess the owner of the United States Stocks upon the retrospective position and value of his property, and not upon its present condition and value, this is a plain and palpable evasion of the National Sovereignty by mere dexterity of State Legislation. With great respect for those who urge such a view, this course cannot be admitted; in the very nature of things, a great fundamental, constitutional, national power cannot be impaired, evaded, or paralysed by legislation of that kind, which is entirely artificial in its character, and refuses to regard things in their true, real, and natural position, and in their actual and vital relations.

The immunity of the General Government in the exercise of its constitutional power to borrow money, from State taxation, is communicable or transmissible. It passes from the government, the borrower, to the individual or corporate lender. Its source and fountain consist in the supremacy of the Constitution and the National Government, whence flow as with a stream all original qualities characterizing the primary source. It is a quality inherent in the exercise of the functions of government, and which secures to that exercise the fullest measure of freedom, in its remotest results and consequences. As the constitution is the supreme law of the land, and every power confided to the general gov-

ernment is beyond all restraint and limit, it has no
boundaries, and no master, through the length and
breadth of the land; and in the single majesty of its
power, it extends its protection to all who trust in its
sovereignty.

In the transaction of loaning to the United States, the
lender in full faith has placed his money in the government coffers, and has received in return from the borrower as security, a pledge to pay. His property is
gone; he has no property in lieu of it except the public
faith thus assured to him; and his immunity from taxation arises from the fact that he has made that loan and
accepted that security on the credit of the United
States, and the guaranties of the Constitution. This
immunity attaches to the security wherever it goes.
It passes from hand to hand, from bank to bank,
from coffer to coffer; wherever that little piece of paper
appears, it carries with it the immunity of the general
government and its creditors from any and every kind
of State imposition, interference, or taxation.

Now, the act in question under which this tax was
levied, if it has any effect whatever, has undertaken to
declare that a bank, which may have its whole capital
and surplus profits invested in government securities,

shall be taxed the same as before; as of a valuation at the time its capital was paid in, or secured to be paid in, including its surplus except ten per cent., and under this direction, the assessors have included in the taxable property of the bank its entire original capital, and its surplus, notwithstanding the bank has loaned the whole capital and surplus to the government of the United States. The State refuses to regard the fact that the capital no longer exists in its original form, and has all been loaned to the United States, but goes back to the remote period when its capital was paid in, or secured to be paid, and taxes what the bank owned then, and no longer owns now; taxes it as of that date, and not of this date. We insist that this cannot be done, without a violation of the Constitution.

SEVENTH. Nor can the privilege of exemption from taxation be independent of the mode of investment. To say that the State does not tax the power to borrow money, nor the credit of the government, nor the evidence of debt in the hands of the lender, but only taxes the lender upon a fixed valuation, without regard to the manner in which his money has been invested, is manifestly equivalent to saying that the mode of investment is indifferent. The answer to this suggestion is, that the tax necessarily falls on the government in whatever way it is levied. The tax affects the value of the stock, and the power to borrow. The government which borrows money subject to taxation, will receive as much per centum from the lender as would nearly equal a capital sufficient to raise an interest equivalent to the rate of taxation (Smith's Wealth of Nations, 2, p. 278), and stock which at par would pay six per cent. interest without taxation, would be worth sixty-six cents on the dollar, if the lender should be obliged to pay a tax of two per cent., supposing the debt perpetually funded. The tax is evidently a direct and immediate impediment to the power of borrowing money. If it reached six per cent. it would exclude the United States from the market.

It is the unfortunate condition of all borrowers, that they pay all the expenses of borrowing. The lender will never lend his money, except upon receiving an adequate return for the employment of his capital, equal to, if not greater than what he would receive if the capital were employed in other modes of investment. This view is elaborated by Mr. Smith, in the place I have noted. Any depreciation always necessarily falls upon the borrower. This is a universal rule, running through the whole range of political economy. The practical effect of this principle may be examined by reference to investments in United States Stock in the city of New York.

The loans redeemable in five or twenty years, known as the five-twenties, pay interest at the rate of six per cent. in gold. The individual lender, who, since the decision of the Supreme Court of the United States, in the cases of The Bank of the Commonwealth and The Bank of Commerce, is certainly free from all taxation, finds here a stock offered to his hand, which produces six per cent. per annum, free from all taxation. The taxes in the city of New York are at present two and a half per cent., with a fair prospect of advancement in the future; and he argues very reasonably : "If I loan upon bond and mortgage, at six per cent. interest, I will have to deduct two and a half or three per cent. for taxes; but if I loan to the government, I will be free from taxation, and will receive six per cent. from my adventure ; I will, therefore, loan to the government." Now suppose the government applies for a loan, subject to State taxation, what would be the result? On a six per cent. loan at par, or one hundred, it takes at least thirty-three per cent. to pay a two per cent. tax, and if it were a perpetual loan, instead of being sold at one hundred, the stock would be reduced to sixty-six. Who bears this loss? The loss falls on the government. Just as the tax is laid or not laid, so the stock rises and falls. The lender is not compelled to loan. The tax makes no difference to him, for in loaning he will give a rate reduced enough to make

up for the tax. When he can get a loan free from taxation at six per cent., he will give one hundred dollars in
money for one hundred dollars in stock ; but if he loans
subject to a tax' of two and a half per cent., the stock is
not worth more than sixty, and that is all that he will
give, and the difference between sixty and one hundred
is to be borne by the government.

So I say that a tax upon United States Stocks in all
cases is a tax upon the Government of the United States,
and upon its means of borrowing money. There is no possible way by which we can escape that conclusion,
because it is the inevitable consequence of the laws of
trade and of political economy, which cannot be affected
or controlled by legislation. It cannot be arranged, or
contrived, that a tax upon securities issued by the government shall fall anywhere but on that government.
The rule is just as certain as the law of gravitation ; it is
governed by universal principles, beyond the reach of
mortal man in any of his efforts, individual or legislative.

This conceded, we must note another important consideration : If the loss falls upon the general government, it is to be paid by the people. This is not a conflict between state sovereignty and the general government, in respect to pecuniary interests. The people have

to bear the loss arising from the tax, and so your
Honors will perceive, that in the end it will amount to
the same thing, regarding the question as a mere matter
of money. Looking at it simply in its pecuniary relations, if the State gain more by taxation of the general
government, and the general government lose, the people have still to pay in some form or another.

It seems to have been forgotten that the people have
two governments to support, the one *national*, and the
other *domestic*. And they must sustain and uphold
these two governments by their property and their
money. And if one of these governments impedes in
any way the operations of the other government, it is
our own agents on the one hand impeding the operations
of our own agents on the other hand; and both governments have in the end to come back to the property
of their people for support and maintenance. If this
year the government of the United States loses a mil-
lion of dollars by reason of State taxation, and the con-
sequent reduction in the value of the securities of the
United States, we shall have to make it up in the end.
It is an utter fallacy to suppose that this is a matter of
pecuniary interest—it is nothing of the kind, but it is a
question of organic power, in respect to a function of the
National Government actually necessary to its existence.

7

There are two methods supplied by the Constitution for obtaining the means of supporting the National Government: One that afforded by taxation, and the other by the power to borrow money on the faith and credit of the United States; the former is ordinarily sufficient in time of peace, the latter is essential in time of war.

The National Constitution was not made for peace only, but also for war. It was planned and adopted by a race of men who had, with a slight intermission, been plunged for many many years into the evils and horrors of two dreadful wars, and who were deeply impressed with all the necessities growing out of a state of continued hostilities, and with the propriety of clothing the government with every possible muniment of power fitted for that condition. It is a Constitution, which upon its face by express terms looks to the possibility of invasion and insurrection, and which, for those purposes, confides the whole power of National Government into the hands of its own chosen officers. It gives that government power to make war and treaties of peace; to coin money, to raise armies and build navies. It contemplated with prophetic vision the probability, if not necessity, of this nation going through the same fiery trials and struggles of war, that have marked the history of other nations so continuously, that it almost seems to be true, that war is the natural condition of man.

Now, the power to tax is in its movements cumbersome and tardy. There are great exigencies in the history of every people, in which it is impossible by the means of taxation alone, to supply the pecuniary resources necessary to meet the emergency. Therefore the power to borrow money was given in addition to the power to tax. It was a separate and independent power, and bestowed for the reason that it affords in a sudden crisis the means of speedily raising sums of money, for which the nation could not wait until the tax-gatherer performed his slow journey.

Where would this government have been at the commencement of the present rebellion, if it had only had power to tax, or only power to borrow money from individuals? When the Secretary of the Treasury came to the city of New York in the spring of 1861, for the purpose of effecting a loan, our country was apparently trembling on the verge of destruction—if he had been limited in efforts to borrow, to the individual capitalists of New York, is it supposable that the requisite amount could have been supplied with promptness? And in September, 1861, when he obtained from the banks of

New York, $150,000,000, what would have been the consequence if the government had been prohibited from borrowing from corporations?

Take all the private capitalists of New York together, and granting the existence of every motive of generosity and patriotism, could they possibly have advanced the money with the requisite speed? But is it certain he would not have been met with cold calculations as to security, and the difficulties of raising money? Put all the capitalists of New York together, outside of the banks, and could they have raised $50,000,000? These questions cannot be answered without admitting that the power to borrow money, and especially to borrow of corporations possessing a great aggregation of capital, is vital to the existence of the government. I suppose that nothing in our recent history is more obvious than that, if at that time the banks of New York had acted grudgingly; if they had not come forward freely, boldly, without consultation with their stockholders, and placed this money at the disposal of the government, the Union would have crumbled into ruins.

If, then, it be a matter of entire *pecuniary* indifference, as between the state and general government, whether this power to borrow be free from State taxation, for the reason that in the end we have to support both governments, and pay both taxes, then I ask why not leave this power to borrow money to the general government, which it is necessary to draw upon as soon as you draw the sword, unimpeded and unimpaired? Why not leave it intact, and declare it, as the Supreme Tribunal has declared it to be, sovereign over all powers, and beyond the reach of State taxation?

EIGHTH. It has been urged, however, in justification of this tax, that "corporations are the mere creatures of the Legislature, which may impose upon them such restrictions and limitations as it pleases for the privileges and advantages which it confers."

If this proposition be sound in all its length and breadth, then it is within State authority to compel a corporation to pay taxes on government securities—a power which it has just been decided by the Supreme Court of the United States, the State does not possess.

If it be repugnant to the Constitution to tax individuals and corporations on Government securities directly, how can it be less so to tax corporations on the ground they are "mere creatures of the Legislature?" To sustain this argument, the sovereignty over a corporation,

because it is a corporation, must be unlimited, and yet it
has been decided by the Supreme Court of the United
States, that it is limited in respect to this very subject,
the power of taxation.

It is not the different guise of the act of legislation, nor
whether it be exercised under one form of sovereignty or
another, which constitutes the rule of exemption or non-
exemption—but the exemption flows from the immunity
of the thing itself—the credit of the United States. " If
it has been shown that stocks of the United States Government cannot be subjected to taxation when owned by
an individual, the rule is necessarily the same when they
are held by a corporation. *The rule is the exemption of
the thing or subject,* and it has no respect to the ownership. There is not one interpretation of the Federal
Constitution when an individual claims exemption under
it, and another one when a corporation makes the same
claim." Comstock J., 23, N. Y. R. p. 192.

In this connection, it is to be observed that the banking associations incorporated under the act of 1838, have
power to lend money to the General Government. This
power is given by State Legislation. They have made
the investment thus authorized, and acquired property
exempt from taxation.

"The suggestion has been made," says Mr. Justice Comstock, "that the Legislature may tax corporations in any mode and to any extent as the price of the privileges and franchises conferred in their charters. This is true as to all subjects to which the taxing power of the State extends. But when a corporation acquires property which is absolutely exempt from all burdens imposed by the States, under the higher authority of the Constitution of the United States, by inevitable logic, such property is acquired and held free from taxation." "The exemption, if it exists at all, is the result of a constitutional principle, which operates in all circumstances, and follows the property wherever it goes." 23, N. Y. R. p. 192.

We deny, however, that the authority of the State over corporations can be exercised so as to become the indirect medium of taxing the credit of the General Government.

This is claimed under the power to alter charters.

That power was reserved for good and beneficent purposes, and for the furtherance of the public welfare. So far as its exercise is made the medium by which unconstitutional objects are sought to be gained, the object of the reservation is transcended. The reservation extends to a full repeal—the same power which could modify the law so as to levy the tax indirectly, could denounce the extinction of the banks if they failed to pay a tax on United States stocks.

If this power be supreme it can levy the tax directly. It cannot be needful to travel through *byways* to exercise its sovereignty.

But that, in respect to the Constitutional powers of the general government, the State has no greater power over corporations than it has over individuals, is manifest from the late decision of this Court in the case of the Metropolitan Bank *vs*. Van Dyck. There the power of the Bank Superintendent to compel payment of bank notes, was held subordinate to the power of the Government to make treasury notes a legal tender. The analogy was recognised, to the immunity of the Government securities from State taxation, declared in the case of the Bank of the Commonwealth, in the United States Supreme Court.

But in the sense of special grants, privileges and franchises, there are no longer any charters, under the General Incorporation Acts of this State.

By the Constitution of 1846, it was provided that:—
"Corporations may be formed under general laws, but
shall not be created by special act, except for municipal
purposes, and in cases where, in the judgment of the
Legislature, the object of the corporation cannot be
attained under general laws. All general laws and
special acts, passed pursuant to this section, may be
altered from time to time or repealed." Art. 8, Sec. 1.

Upon this change in the organic law, it became obvious that the idea of special franchises, except in particular cases, had been abandoned. Corporations were no
longer esteemed as the recipients of special grants, or
royalties, but simply as bodies, coming into existence by
their own volition under general laws for the benefit of
the State. They were subjects of favor and approbation,
and justly regarded as objects of encouragement. Their
creation was invited, not conceded. They were recognised as the great engines of modern civilization, presenting a combination of capital, skill, and labor for the
benefit of all the industrial, commercial, and benevolent
interests of society.

The Legislature of 1847, acting in harmony with the
spirit of this section of the Constitution, provided as follows: "All individual bankers, and all banking associa-

tions, which are now, or *shall be hereafter*, engaged in the
business of banking, under the provisions of the act entitled 'An Act to authorise the business of banking,' shall
be subject to taxation on the full amount of actual capital paid in, or secured to be paid in, as such capital,
severally, *at the actual market value* of such securities, to
be estimated by the Comptroller, without any deduction
for the debts of such individual banker or banking association." Laws 1847.

3. At an early period in the legislation of this State,
a discrimination was made between manufacturing corporations and other corporations. This discrimination
originated as early as the year 1817, when the "American System" was in vogue, and when it was thought wise
and patriotic to encourage domestic manufactures.

The preference in favor of this class of companies was
indicated—1. By allowing them to be formed under
general acts of incorporation. 2. By taxing them only
upon the *actual value* of their stock. (The People *vs.*
The Utica Ins. Co., 15 J. R., 382 ; The Columbian Manufacturing Co. *vs.* Vanderpoel, 4 Cowen, 557 ; The Bank
of Utica *vs.* The City of Utica, 4 Paige, 402 ; The Union
Cotton Manufacturing Co. *vs.* The Supervisors of Oneida,
1 Barb. Ch. R., 448.)

When, by the mandate of the Constitution, the Legislature was called upon to pass general acts of incorporation, and was forbidden to grant special charters, except for municipal purposes, etc., it seemed proper to place the banks, then existing, under the act of 1838, on the same footing as manufacturing companies; and this no doubt led to the provision of the act of 1847, taxing the banks upon the market value of their capital.

In 1853, another change took place approximating the mode of taxing corporations to that of individuals. All corporations were made taxable on surplus profits, exceeding ten per cent. (Laws of 1853, Ch. 654, p. 1240.)

Finally by the act of 1857, all distinctions in respect to corporations, however, or for whatsoever purpose created, were swept away. The provisions of the revised statutes relating to the taxation of manufacturing, turnpike and marine Insurance companies were repealed, and all corporations were made taxable on the "*actual value*" of capital, except so much as might be "*exempted by law*," and the capital was directed to be "*taxed in the same manner as the other personal and real estate of the county.* (Laws, 1857, Ch. 456.")) (Sections 7, 11, 12, 13, of title 4, 1 R. S. 414, were repealed by Ch. 634,

Laws, 1853. Sections, 9, 10 14 were repealed by Ch. 456, Laws, 1857.)

We may justly conclude then from the whole tenor of the State Legislation, and from the Constitution of 1846, that there is no countenance to be given to the idea of any special favor, or act of royalty in the creation of corporations. They receive nothing from Legislative bounty for which they are bound to pay. They come into existence by general statutes, and by the will of the people expressed in the organic law.

They are subjects of the taxing power, the same as individuals, upon the general ground of State sovereignty, and not by reason of being recipients of Legislative favor.

The act of the Legislature now under consideration, if held to operate as an effective tax on the banks, is liable to another grave objection.

From the passage of the act of 1857 to April 1863, a period of six years, the banks were exempt from taxation on funds loaned to the United States, whatever may have been the just construction of the statutes previous to 1857. (*Dolloway* vs. *The Oswego Starch Factory*, 21 N. Y. R. 449.)

The banks had previously to 1863, under State authority (Laws, 1840, Ch. 313 ; Laws of 1849, Ch. 313,) been invited to purchase Government securities. They had in full view of the immunity from taxation, under the Constitution of the United States, and under the Constitution and laws of this State, loaned large amounts to the General Government, sustaining its finances during a period of great pressure.

Confessedly these securities now held were acquired during a period from 1857, when, by the method of taxation, they were exempt. This exemption was a vested right, and cannot be impaired by any State law subsequently enacted. *Dodge* vs. *Woolsey*, 18 Howard, 330.

Ninth. Whatever may have been the intention or design of the Act of 1863, it is so framed that in its force and effect, and practical operation, it has not changed the system of State taxation, but has left it as it previously existed—a tax on property.

The Act of April, 1863, applies only to " Banks, Banking Associations, and other Moneyed Corporations, and Associations." It leaves other corporations to be taxed under the Law of 1857. It relates simply to moneyed institutions—the only class of corporations likely to invest in Government securities. Taking this in view, as well as the time and occasion of its passage, there would seem to be no doubt of its object. At the moment of its passage the Supreme Court had recently declared these institutions exempt from taxation on the securities of the United States to whom money had been loaned to the amount of many hundred millions of dollars.

But the effect of the law must be deduced from its language and its relations to the system of which it is an integral part.

It will not be denied that it is a cardinal rule in the interpretation of statutes, that they are to be construed, so far as possible, in harmony with existing statutes, *in pari materia*, not expressly repealed ; that they are to be construed, so far as possible, in harmony with the constitutional duty of the Legislature—in respect both to the organic law of the State, and of the United States ; and that effect is to be given to their provisions only so far as they are not in conflict with the provisions of the organic law, as interpreted by the appropriate · tribunal.

While I insist there can be no doubt of the hostile intent of this Act, still I submit that the object has wholly failed, for the reason that the act is a mere graft upon the general Legislation of the State in respect to taxes, which still remains in all its features a system of taxation *on property.*

In the application of the rules which I have just stated we find that the act in question deals only with "*taxation.*" It is entitled "An Act in Relation to the *Taxation* of Moneyed Corporations and Associations," and declares they "shall be liable to *taxation,* on a *valuation,* equal to the amount of their *capital stock,* paid in or secured to be paid in, and their surplus earnings (less ten per cent. of such surplus)."

It will be observed, also, that no special mode is provided for raising the tax, but the tax is directed to be levied "*in the manner now provided by law.*" So that the entire body of the existing law on the subject of taxation is to be taken as intact and operative, except so far as disturbed by the new act; and so that in order to levy the tax, and ascertain its subject, we are referred to the Revised Statutes, by the tenor of which it is only property that is taxable; by the express language of which all property exempt under the *Constitution of the United States* is declared exempt: And to the law of 1857, which provides that: "*The capital stock* of every company liable to *taxation*, except such part of it as has been excepted in the assessment roll, or as shall have been *exempted by law*, together with its reserved profits or reserved funds exceeding ten per cent. of its capital, after deducting the assessed value of its real estate, and all shares of other corporations actually owned by such company, which are taxable on their capital stock under the law of this State, shall be assessed at its actual value, and taxed in the same manner as the other real and personal estate of the county."

And we must also have recourse to the Act of 1859, the very law by which these Commissioners were constituted, under which they made their assessment, and which requires their deputies " to assess all the taxable *property*" in their several districts, from which the Commissioners are to make up "the annual record of the assessed valuation of *real and personal estate*," from which the assessment rolls are copied.

Supposing there was no intention to conflict with the ruling of the Supreme Court of the United States in the tax cases decided immediately before the passage of this law, and its legitimate consequences, we might construe the act as in harmony with the existing law thus wise—

Monied corporations shall be taxable on their property, real and personal, as follows:

On real estate, at its actual value.

On capital paid in or secured to be paid in, at a valuation equal to its original amount, deducting—

(1.) The assessed value of their real estate.

(2.) All property exempt by law, or under the Constitution of the United States.

(3.) Shares of other corporations taxable on their capital stock.

(4.) Amount of stock held by the State, or by charitable or literary institutions.

The exemption contained under the second subdivision is reached by reference to the decision of the Supreme Court of the United States, and also the exemption declared under first title of Ch. XIII. of the Revised Statutes.

Now, it is remarkable that the tax commissioners *have allowed these exemptions,* so far as they relate to shares

in other corporations, and stock owned by charitable
and literary institutions, but have *rejected* the exemption
in favor of the United States. The former stood alone
under the protection of the State law ; the latter, under
the protection of the State law : and of the Constitution
of the United States, a law of Congress, and a decision
of the Supreme Court, which are the supreme law of the
land.

Again, the Commissioners return that they have
assessed " *the actual value*" of the stock. This is in obe-
dience to the law of 1857. They determined, they say,
" the actual value of the said capital stock," and they
maintain that the bank, being a corporation, is liable to
State burdens, and, " among other burdens, it is, and was
at the time of such assessment, subject to assessment
and taxation upon the *value* of its capital stock, without
regard to the fact that such capital stock, or any portion
of it, might be invested in the public stocks, debts or
bonds of the United States, and that such assessment was
not made upon the public stocks or bonds of the United
States, but was made pursuant to the laws of said State
of New York, upon the capital stock of said bank,
estimated at its *just value, making the exceptions
and deductions required by the statutes of said
State.*"

These exceptions and deductions required by the statutes of said State are those contained in the First Title of Ch. XIII., 1st part of the Revised Statutes.

The same statute exempted property from taxation which is exempt UNDER THE CONSTITUTION OF THE UNITED STATES.

On what ground, then, and under what color of authority, could the Commissioners have allowed the former, and rejected the latter. Is one class of exceptions preferable over another ? Is one more sacred than the other ?

The law of 1857 required an assessment of the *actual value* of the stock, the same as other personal estate in the county.

The law of 1863 calls for a valuation equal to the amount of the original stock.

Between these two, the Commissioners seem to have been in a state of perplexity.

They return that they assessed the actual value. This actual value could only have been ascertained by looking into the *investments* of the capital and the surplus ; and

yet they repudiate any regard to the mode of investment, and adopt a valuation equivalent to the original
capital, and the amount of surplus.

To escape all these difficulties and inconsistencies, and
in order to construe the law of 1863 in harmony with
pre-existing statutes, and with Constitutional require-
ments, it should be read as making liable to taxation, at
a valuation equal to its original amount, only so much of
the capital as is *not exempt* by other provisions of law,
or under the Constitution of the United States. Thus,
if in the case of a bank having a capital of $500,000, a
part, say $100,000, is invested in United States stocks,
$50,000 is owned by literary and charitable institutions,
and $50,000 is in the stock of other corporations liable to
taxation, the remaining $300,000, after making these
deductions, can be rated at its original amount.

In this there would be no transgression of the Constitution of the United States.

TENTH. But, if it be true that the Act of 1863 was
intended to effect a taxation of the entire amount of the
capital of a bank, whether invested in loans to the general government or not, then we claim that the act was
framed and passed with the intention to avoid the force

and effect of the decision of the Supreme Court of the United States.

Such an evasion could only be attempted by *indirection*. If the act had declared expressly that stocks of the United States should be taxed, or that banks were taxable on so much of their capital as was invested in securities of the United States, the act would most clearly have been void upon its face. At the time of the passage of the act, and when the tax was levied, the capital and surplus, or most of it, was invested in these securities. As property they existed in no other shape.

It is manifest, therefore, that the banks could not be assessed upon the property which they *actually had*.

And yet it is only upon the property which one *has*, that a tax can be levied under the general law.

To alter the basis of taxation, therefore, it was requisite to change it from present property to past property.

And then we would have this result, that the immunity of the power of the Government to borrow money, from State taxation, can be avoided, by taxing the lender for what he had before he made the loan.

And we meet the further difficulty, that, under statutes professing to tax property existing at the time of taxation, a tax can be levied upon property passed and gone, no longer in the possession of the tax-payer, but in the possession of the Government—the only property the tax-payer has, being the securities of the Government.

The act in question seems, on the supposition the construction sought to be given it is correct, to have been framed under a sense of this difficulty.

It provides that monied corporations shall be taxable on—what ?—not property—but on "a valuation"—a valuation of what? Nothing—"on a valuation equal to the amount of their capital stock, paid in, or secured to be paid in," etc.

If the act had provided they should be taxable on a "valuation of their property," it would have been repugnant to the decision of the Supreme Court of the United States—and so these corporations are made taxable simply on "a valuation" of nothing.

We cannot deal with Constitutional rights in this light way. This act is an old foe with a new face. We are to regard substance, not forms. The moment before this act was passed, the stocks of the United States held by the banks were free from taxation, as decided by the Supreme Court—the moment after, these securities were no longer exempt, as decided by the Tax Commissioners; and this change has been effected by State Legislation.

As with a dexterous fencer, a slight turn of the wrist may change an innocuous blow to a vital wound, so this Legislation assumes, that by levying a tax on a nominal amount, the effect of a Constitutional immunity can be avoided. Present property cannot be taxed, because invested in Government securities. Original property cannot be taxed, because no longer held in possession: but you shall be taxed on a valuation. Can anything be more vague, indefinite, and meaning-less? Like those misty figures which arise out of caverns, in the Arabian Nights, it presents a form with the appearance of substance, without its reality. Now, what do we understand by valuation? In valuing a thing, we determine what it is worth in exchange; exchange for sheep, horses, gold, silver, or currency. But it is a real thing, not a fictitious, shadowy nonentity; and the valuation is not arbitrary, but depends upon the fact, whether some other thing that is valuable can be had in exchange for the thing valued.

But the act in question omits to say what it is that is valued. The tax is laid on a valuation " equal to," not " of "—*equal to* the amount of the capital stock, and surplus, etc. Now, if grave Constitutional privileges and rights can be escaped by that kind of verbal machinery, by substituting words for things, then the powers of the general government are necessarily at the mercy of the State Legislators.

CHIEF JUSTICE DENIO.—Is not the word " valuation" equivalent to the word "sum" or " amount ?"

MR. BRADFORD.—" Sum " or " amount," if so intended, would not mean anything that is present, but would be referable to the past, to the amount which was once there, but which is now gone. Your Honors will recollect that it is property which we are speaking of, and it is present property. There is nothing in the tax law by which an individual is taxed upon the property which he *has* had—that would be monstrous. The State taxes the individual upon the property which he *now* has, and . the only property which these banks have is their capital, and that capital has been paid over to the general government, and the substitutes for it are the securities given by the general government. So that the only property which these banks *now have* are the securities of

the general government. And to escape the privilege
of the banks to be free from a tax upon the property
which they now have, the Legislature resorts to the
scheme of taxing the property which they now *have not*,
but which they had years ago, and have loaned to the
United States.

ELEVENTH. The idea of a tax upon "Capital Stock," as
a thing distinct from the property actually owned by
the banks, is not well founded. It was upon this position the case was placed by the learned judge, Mr. Justice
Sutherland, who gave the opinion at the General Term,
and not upon the construction of the word valuation,
holding that the taxing of the capital of a bank looks
to some other thing than the property in which that
capital is invested; that the property in which the capital of the bank is invested is one thing, and the capital
stock is another thing, and you may tax the capital of
the bank, although it is invested in property not taxable.
The learned judge, also, maintained that this, which was
the original ground he took at the Special Term, in the
case of The Bank of the Commonwealth in 1859, and
which was adhered to by Mr. Justice Bonney, in the
General Term, but which was not admitted in this court,
is still the right ground, and he rests the case upon that
proposition. I admit, in its fullest extent, the sovereign

10

power of the Legislature of the State over corporations, whether formed under special or general laws; except so far as impairing the obligation of contracts. But although the State may lay a tax upon franchises, yet, whenever such tax upon franchises in any way infringes upon this right of immunity from taxation of the stock of the general government, so far it is a conflict of State Sovereignty with the Sovereignty of the General Government. And I deny the general proposition, that because corporations are the creatures of the Legislature, the State can exercise any sovereign power over their property, which in regard to individuals it could not exercise, whenever such act comes in conflict with the power of the United States to borrow money. In other words, I admit that the State can tax the franchise to any imaginable extent; but in doing so this property of the corporation invested in Government securities must continue to be exempt; whenever the tax comes in conflict with this right of exemption, the latter must prevail over all State Sovereignty, in whatever channel or by whatever mode exercised.

Moreover I maintain that the capital of a bank differs in no sense from that of an individual, or copartnership. It is necessarily fixed at some sum, and the interests of the several corporators are represented by shares. But the capital itself is the property of the corporation. And we find, accordingly, the words " capital," " capital stock," and " property," used indiscriminately, in the statutes relating to the taxation of corporations.

If, however, the *capital stock* of a bank is something else other than its property, it becomes a matter of no moment how it is valued—whether at actual or nominal values. Its being the subject of taxation, arises from its existence as a different thing from the property owned by the bank.

So, if it is not a different thing, but the same thing, then it is not the subject of State taxation, if the property in which it consists is not such subject.

But the conclusive reply to this proposition is afforded by the decisions of this Court in the tax cases, and the Supreme Court of the United States on appeal, where no countenance is given to the idea.

It follows from the previous considerations, therefore, that treating the tax as really a tax upon the *present* property of the banks, there must of necessity be deducted from the aggregate, all securities of the United States, and this plain duty cannot be avoided either by treating the term " capital " as meaning something different from the property in which it is invested, or by assessing the capital at a nominal amount independently of its mode of investment. In either of the latter alternatives the public securities are taxed.

The argument is put in another form, by saying it is the institutions which are taxed, and not the property. In addition to what has been urged, I maintain that the institutions cannot be taxed in the mode proposed when such mode leads to an actual though indirect taxation of United States Stocks.

The institutions acquired their securities under a state of the law which exempted the securities from taxation, and if no longer exempt, it is obvious that the change has been effected by some act of State Sovereignty.

The right to control corporations cannot be wielded successfully for such a purpose, any more than the right to control individuals.

If these institutions exist at the will of the Legislature, while they do exist, they cannot be made the medium of taxing the general government. All the functions of

State Sovereignty, whether the power to tax, to license, to create and alter the powers and duties of corporations—all are subordinate to the supremacy of the Constitution of the United States.

Suppose a preamble to the act in question reciting the history of this controversy, as follows: "Whereas, by an act of the Legislature of the State of New York, passed in the year 1857, banking corporations were taxed only upon the actual value of their capital stock.

"And whereas, in the year 1859, the Bank of the Commonwealth claimed exemption from taxation on so much of its capital as was invested in loans of the United States, and such claim was adjudged invalid in the Courts of the State of New York, but on appeal to the Supreme Court of the United States, was declared lawful and valid; and it was further adjudged by said Supreme Court that stocks of the United States are not the subject of State taxation, but are to be deducted from the aggregate of the tax-payer's property before taxation.

"Therefore, be it enacted that all banks, banking associations, etc., 'shall be liable to taxation on a valuation equal to the amount of the capital stock, etc.'"

Thus we should find, if the change from *actual* to *nominal* values be allowed as affecting the subjects of taxation, substituting institutions for property, by a single stroke, the credit of the United States declared by the highest tribunal *not to be taxable*, successfully taxed under a State law, passed within a few weeks after the decision was pronounced.

What is a *nominal* valuation? Simply one that is not *real*, but artificial—verbal—a *nomen*.

Can a great Constitutional right be dependent upon names. " Is the proposition to be maintained that the Constitution meant to prohibit names and not things," is the inquiry of Marshall.—4 Peters' R., 433.

If, then, by a *nominal* or arbitrary valuation, a result is produced which is *real*, and which could not have been effected on an *actual* valuation, we reach the conclusion that while the powers of the Government cannot be assailed directly, they may be indirectly, and as fully and lawfully as if assailed directly. This cannot be.

TWELFTH. There is no conflict in principle or interest between the United States and the State Governments upon this subject.

First—As to the principle involved, it must be conceded that all the Constitutional means which the Government of the United States is authorized to employ for National purposes are in derogation of State authority, and these means are necessarily reserved from the interference, legislation, and dominion of the States. Otherwise they might be defeated or impeded. The principle of the exemption of the credit of the Government from State taxation, is based upon the national sovereignty and the supremacy of the Constitution, by a direct grant of power from the people, and from the States. In this grant the people of New York and the State of New York in its corporate capacity, were grantors, and parted with or conceded a portion of their power. In this respect we have two Constitutions, one for domestic and the other for National purposes. The former is supreme over its subjects, the latter is subordinate in respect to all the subjects of the former. As the preservation of the general government is of paramount consideration, and its Constitutional acts have been made SUPREME, the first duty is to sustain the National Constitution within the scope of its functions and powers.

Second—As to the interest of the State, it cannot be denied that the power of borrowing money is essential to the continuance of the Government. It is a vital ele-

ment of the national existence. It should not only be
left untouched and untrammelled, but should be aided
and promoted. People and States are all interested
alike in the support of the general government, as well
as in the support of the state governments, and all are
bound to contribute to the maintenance of both.

The idea seems to have prevailed, that by loaning
money to the general government clothed with immunity from taxation, a vast amount will be withdrawn
from the taxable property of the State, and the financial
resources of the State thus be impaired.

A loan of money to the Government, ordinarily
abstracts nothing from the capital of the community.
The money is not hoarded, but is returned within a brief
period to the active industry of the country. It is not
in fact taken from the taxable property, for although the
lender cannot be taxed on the money which is no longer
his, the money itself has passed into other hands and
still remains the subject of taxation. If one hundred
millions of money owned by the banks of New York, be
loaned to the Government, and be disbursed by the
Government to its creditors in New York, the property
has only changed hands, and remains taxable the same
as before it was loaned. If it were carried abroad, or if

hoarded by the Government, then it would be abstracted from the working capital of the country. Within a few days, if not hours, after a loan is effected, and the money received, it finds its way from the National Treasury through a thousand different rills, as the blood sent to the heart through the veins is again diffused through the system by the arteries.

The $1,200,000,000 borrowed by the Government have been paid to the soldiers in the field, to artificers, ship-builders, etc., for supplies of food, clothing, munitions of war, and have been restored through numerous channels, into the mass of the taxable property of the States.

The State tax is an illustration of the law of return. As much property and money remain in the State after the tax is levied and disbursed, as there was before— Smith's Wealth of Nations, 2, p. 272.

In this law we see the reason why the country has been able to borrow, and capitalists able to loan, the enormous sums expended in the present war.

How could banks having a capital of only $95,000,000, have loaned many times their capital to the United States, had it not been that the very money which was paid by the banks to the Government to-day, was returned to the banks the next day by its own depositors who had received it from the Government? The hands of the cashier or the teller, who pays the money out to the United States, are hardly through the process of counting before it comes back again from the depositors who have received it from the Government. Now, if the money is returned, if besides taxing the 1,200,000,000 of money borrowed by the Government, and restored to the taxable property of the State, a tax is laid, also, upon the $1,200,000,000 of Government securities, then we shall have a tax twice levied; we shall tax capitalists double, taxing first the money loaned and returned, and then again the securities. It is, therefore, clearly a fallacy, to suppose that by the process of loaning on securities exempt from taxation, anything is permanently withdrawn from the taxable property of the State.

I have had the curiosity, in view of these great financial operations of the Government, and the manner in which they have been aided and supported in the city of New York, to examine the returns of the Tax Commissioners during the period of the present war, and though the material thus afforded can never be entirely satisfactory, by reason of several considerations, yet it shows a startling fact entirely in consonance with the view I have advanced; that by loaning to the Government, capital is not abstracted from the community. Your Honors are aware of the general extent of these loans: they have amounted in New York to the extent of three or four millions a day, and latterly, principally from individuals' because the capital of the banks was long since all absorbed in the loans to the Government. The very first effort to support the Government, in its death agony as it were, withdrew their capital from all the banks. The consequence is, that although the subsequent loans were effected through the medium of the banks, the banks had instantly to spread the amount among their customers and the community at large. It is safe to say, the Southern States being excluded, that the cities of Philadelphia, New York, and Boston, have mainly contributed to negotiating the loans of the Government, and that the greater part of the loans have been taken in New York. Now, where the individual loans, he is exempt from taxation, and this has always been admitted by the Tax Commissioners, or assessors, in every State. Then on a fair calculation, several hundred millions of dollars, to say the least, must have been loaned to the Government by the capitalists of New York, outside of the banks. Now, if the argument were true, that that money was abstracted from the taxable capital of the State of New York, it would be demonstrable there.

If it be true that the money loaned by our citizens to the Government has been taken away from the taxable capital of the city, and has not been returned again, we should find evidence of the fact upon the tax lists.

But on examining these lists it appears that the total value of the taxable property of the city of New York, for the years 1860, 1861, 1862, and 1863, is rated as follows: For 1860, the taxable property was rated at $576,-621,000; in 1861, at $581,000,000; in 1862, at $571,-000,000, and in 1863, it rose to $594,000,000. Real estate during the whole period has remained nearly the same. In 1860, real estate was valued at $397,000,000; in 1861, at $406,000,000; in 1862, at $399,000,000, and in 1863, at $402,000,000.

But personal property, which, under the idea that taxable capital has been abstracted from the community, by reason of immunity from taxation, should have decreased, is shown to be as follows: In 1861, $174,000,-000; in 1862, $172,000,000. Now we come to the period in which the exemption from taxation has been made active and effective by the operation of the laws of the United States, and the decision of the Supreme Court of the United States. In 1863, the personal estate amounted to $192,000,000, being an increase of $20,000,000 in one year. So that I say that it is clearly demonstrated that the effect of the loans to the Government is in no way to be considered as producing an abstraction from the taxable property of the State; but on the contrary the public debt rather contributes to the expansion of the trade and commerce of the country, and the increase of its taxable capital.

Finally, and in a measure to recapitulate, we urge that while there is ultimately no conflict of sovereignty, or of interest, on this subject, between the State and its people, and the United States, it cannot be overlooked that the power to borrow money was given by the Constitution, to meet all the exigencies of Government, and although the people have eventually to bear all burdens by the process of taxation, that process is necessarily tardy. When revolutions are impending, the arbitrament of the sword is invoked, fleets are to be built and equipped, and great armies are to be raised and armed, there is no time to wait for the tax-gatherer.

The Constitution was designed as the perpetual basis of a great Government, and the powers vested in its ministers were intended for all the emergencies, trials and perils which might occur through all time. It contemplated insurrection, invasion, and war; and its provisions were so framed, in the masterly wisdom of statesmanship and profound political philosophy, as to impart every function necessary to the efficiency and vigor of a National Government.

The power to borrow money on the faith and credit of the United States, has no superior. Without its possession this Government would perish. It should therefore be cherished. It was granted deliberately by all the people, and should be sustained rather than impeded by State authority. Neither mode nor form, nor scheme, nor plan can be countenanced, which in any measure or degree, directly or indirectly, immediately or remotely, interferes with the full and uncontrolled exercise of this power, or with the pledges of faith given by the United States in pursuance of it, or with the persons, bodies or corporations who have accepted those pledges, and contributed their property to the Government.

If the broad and firm ground of principle upon which is based entire immunity from State control of all the means of Government within the scope of the Constitution, be impaired or taken away in this State, under one mode, in other States in other modes; the National

Government will be in danger of constant conflicts with the States.

There is no middle ground of safety, or of sound construction. There must be entire exemption, or subjection to taxation.

www.ingramcontent.com/pod-product-compliance
Lightning Source LLC
Chambersburg PA
CBHW031451270326
41930CB00007B/945